Only Here

Only Here

SELECTED POEMS BY
JOE SALERNO

with an Afterword by Donald Hall

An Ars Poetica Book
Skylands Writers and Artists Association, Inc.

Library of Congress Catalog Card Number: 98-71250

ISBN 1-886841-07-1

Book design by Janet Pedersen/Tenth Street Productions

Manufactured in the United States of America
by Thomson-Shore, Inc.

An Ars Poetica Book

an imprint of
Skylands Writers and Artists Association, Inc.
Post Office Box 15
Andover, New Jersey 07821-0015

Distributed By
ARS POETICA
Post Office Box 866
Lake Hopatcong, NJ 07849-0866

To Beverly

Acknowledgements

Some of these poems originally appeared as they are printed here
or in slightly different forms in the following publications:
*Abraxis, Black Swan Review, Blue Unicorn, Crab Creek Review,
Green House, Journal of New Jersey Poets, Michigan Quarterly Review,
Midwest Poetry Review, Poet and Critic, Portable Wall, Psychopoetica,
Seneca Review, Sun / Father Journal, Windless Orchard,
Wormwood Review, Yankee Magazine.*

Grateful acknowledgement is also made to the Geraldine R. Dodge
Foundation for hosting a Memorial Reading for Joe Salerno in the Willow
Tent at the 1996 Geraldine R. Dodge Poetry Festival at Waterloo Village,
and to Jean Harper and McKeown's Restaurant for hosting a publication
reading for Joe's first book, *Dream Paintings from the Heaven of Obscurity*, in
April 1997. Finally, the Editorial Board expresses its sincere thanks to
Skylands Writers and Artists Association and its President, Daniela
Gioseffi, for their numerous and significant contributions to all aspects of
this project.

The Friends of Joe Salerno

Below is a list, in the order contributions were received, of the Friends of Joe Salerno, who responded generously to the call for donations to make possible publication of Joe Salerno's books *Only Here* and *Dream Paintings from the Heaven of Obscurity*. An asterisk denotes benefactors who have made major contributions. Double asterisks denote Editorial Board members who have helped steer this project from the beginning. Triple asterisks indicate both.

Ben Parra

Newton Abdalla

Linda Scherb

David Jarrin

Tony Gruenewald

Toni Wisman

Nathan Shashoua

B. J. Ward

Rich Mauro

Marcus C. Donisi

Nancy King

Michael Bugeja

Joan Rozgonyi

Jim Snyder

Barbara & Steve Milligan

Isabel D. Emmerich

Ray & Gloria Leppanen

*Bob & Deb Erickson

Franklin Klein

Susan Marlett

*Joram Heilbronner

*Liz Toronto

*Roger W. Miller

Susan Rau

*Marjorie Baird Weber

*Chin-Yeh & Wen-Wen Chi

Steven Domenicucci

Gad Gruenstein

Adele Kenny

**Edie Eustice

***Joe Weil

***Deborah C. LaVeglia

**Catherine Doty

**Daniela Gioseffi

Renee Ashley

David A. Heinlein

Dan Serebrakian

O. L. Beckwith

Ed & Bea Lhotak

Rosemary Meier

Rogan Kelly

Jim & Jean Scharf

Phebe Davidson

*Ken Wisman

Rob & Lisa Goldstein

Larry Blessman

Rita C. Del Pizzo

*Mr. & Mrs. Richard Valera

Charlie Mosler

*Florence Phillips

*Elsie Boehm

*Sam Friedman

*Eleanor Sorensen

*John Pastore

Michael R. Snyder

Istvan &Wimberly Mohos

Linda Jaekel Seils

Kenneth Brown

Karen L. McGregor

*Joseph L. Rich

Thomas J. Obrzut

Steve & Linda Pollock

Brett Kuehner

*Peggy & Bob La Rotonda

*Object Solutions, Inc.

Gina & John Larkin

Jennifer Watts

Richard Cerruto

Anne Wright

Laurence Goldstein

Peter Lomax

Paul D. Aronoff

Herb & Mika Applebaum

Gene & John Thomas

Albion Urdank

Dan Heilbronner

*Peter Serchuk

Madeline Tiger

Thomas Rose

***Donald Hall

Shelley Benaroya

*Rene Haas

*Paul McFarlane

Edward & Roberta Cifelli

*Lou Salerno & Herman McDowell

Harriet Lefkowith

Mark Hillringhouse

Marilyn & Steve Mohr

Lee Brenner

Barbara Wind

Nancy Swann

Ric & Royane Mosley

*Philip &Virginia Leppanen

Jeff Justin

Lydia Cerini

Beth Borrus

Esther E. Sorensen

Laura Pavy

Cathy & Charles Lachmann

Kristen Leppanen

***Sander & Madeline Zulauf

Joan Cusack Handler

Ken Hart

Ellen Bucciarelli

Joanne Herb

Al Balaskovits

Jean & Bob Bader

John & Teresa Carson

Rick & Lilly Stanton

Michael Dermansky

S. William Zulauf

Marge Mueller

Joseph Ogando

Kenneth M. Brown

***David Tucker

Angela Salerno

Anne C. Wallace

Contents

Introduction

When Joe Salerno died on November 22, 1995, at age forty-nine, he had been writing poems almost every day for more than thirty years. On and around his desk in the basement of his home in North Caldwell, New Jersey, there were at least ten distinct manuscripts containing hundreds of poems: collections of narrative and lyrical verse, a book of 120 pages of haiku, a book of poems about work, a manuscript written under a pseudonym in which the poet purports to be a medieval Chinese water colorist, and a series of poems by a Kerouackian character calling himself Jack Sumac.

The ambition and amount of Joe's work would be only a curiosity, if not for the fact that he was such a terrific poet for so long. If this is your first encounter with his poetry, you are about to make gratifying discoveries. He was a poet of tough technical grace whose imagination was always up to something daring and wonderful. In the following pages you will meet a snail sipping a molecule from the trough of a leaf, a dominatrix wearing a blue wasp on her finger, hear an earthworm singing, tour a heaven of nachos, whisky and cigarettes, and encounter an hysterical baldheaded man who dances in a rain of falling hair. These creatures and images inhabit a manuscript Joe was putting together before he died.

Joe's poetry was varied—playful, sad, mystical, incredibly funny. Many voices spoke in many moods and rhythms, but some themes were fairly consistent. He celebrated things that were broken, battered, obscure, tiny, modest, threatened, powerless. He wrote about the mundane as if it were exotic, always trying to break through to the life that is hidden from us, yet near. Woodlice under an old log, the dragonfly that enters from the open window, the weed bulb covered with snow, are sending out faint signals to the soul, if we are listening. He celebrated the unexpected moments of peace; he was always working toward affirmation, and joy. Though he was preoccupied with the life of the spirit, Joe's poems travel on the five senses. He wrote fabulous poems about sex but vibrant sensuality was a part of almost all of his poetry. His Bull God, grazing mindlessly in the summer heat, is one of the most heathen animals in American literature:

> He waits for the next flutter of delight
> to stir the heavy neurons of his brain
> and start again the oblivious lumbering
> from pleasure to pleasure. The long
> slow nerve of his body touched
> by the scent of bulrushes and black mud

Joe was a gentle enemy of self-importance, vanity and worldly success in most of its forms. He liked failure, the idea of it. He thought the word was beautiful and used it often in his poems. And though he had a "successful" career as a technical writer for computer companies, he disliked work intensely; his poems sing the joys of being laid off, the pleasures of sick days, the happiness of doing nothing in an empty house. Poetry, he writes,

> is the art of not succeeding.
> The art of making a little ritual
> out of your own bad luck, lighting a little fire
> made of leaves, reciting a prayer
> in the ordinary dark.

Joe was writing strong poems even back in his student days during the early 1970s at the University of Michigan, where he was one of the stars in a remarkable group of young poets all on campus at the same time. The scene included Jane Kenyon, Larry Josephs, Gregory Orr, Mary Baron, Lawrence Raab, Shelly Siegel, Peter Serchuk, and many others. Most of the youngsters met and exchanged poems in the classes and workshops of poet Donald Hall, then a professor at Michigan and the chief mentor in a faculty flush with teacher-poets, Robert Hayden, Laurence Goldstein, Lemuel Johnson and Radcliffe Squires among them.

Joe did not publish a book in his lifetime, a fact readers will find remarkable once they know his poetry. He won the Hopwood Award for his poetry while at Michigan. He published more than sixty poems in magazines. His poems appeared in several anthologies, he read on radio broadcasts, received arts council grants and gave hundreds of readings. But his pursuit of a book publisher was nonchalant and mostly limited to the yearly crapshoot of poetry contests. He saw no reason to hurry.

He would probably want to be remembered for his poems about family and friends. He was passionately married to Beverly Salerno—a marriage he celebrated with dozens of tender, adoring, unsentimental love poems—and he made his three children the center of his life. He also made friendships by the hundreds. People were drawn to his modesty, his wild humor and his disarming interest in the smallest details of their lives. And he maintained and tended friendships with relentless devotion, continuing long letter-writing relationships with those who moved on.

Joe died of a fast-moving cancer. A lump was discovered on his back in July of 1995, and on the day before Thanksgiving he was gone. He was never bitter. He regretted only that he could not have spent more time with his children. At his memorial service, the church was jammed to the rafters with his family, friends and with poets who admired him. They read his poems all afternoon, into the evening.

In the months since he died, friends and fellow poets have made the publication of Joe's work a cause. The tireless, passionate efforts of members of the Skylands Writers and Artists Association of New Jersey, most particularly of poets Sander Zulauf and Joe Weil, led to the publication of Joe's first book, the chapbook *Dream Paintings from the Heaven of Obscurity,* in early 1997. This same group spearheaded the publication of this manuscript. Donald Hall gave invaluable help and advice at many key points along the way.

—David Tucker

Only Here

IN THE HEAVEN OF OBSCURITY

In heaven, no one will be famous, not even for fifteen minutes

Sure it's quiet
but it's paradise none-the-less.
Look around, there's all this room
to stretch out, relax, watch a little
television. There are no obstacles
here, as you can see, nothing
to overcome if you don't want to.
No "public" clamoring for an encore.
No one pounding on your door shouting
"Five more minutes, Mr. Famous!"
Over there, on the table,
there's whisky and dates and rich
dark chocolate all for you. Help yourself
right now if you want. Or just sit,
take your glasses off and rub
the bridge of your nose before laying back
your head on this soft pillow—
There's all the time in the world now
for nothing to happen. If you listen
closely, you can hear the faint singing
of gnats as you fall asleep.

Or if you'd rather, step outside
and walk around. The view is wonderful—
miles and miles of wind and dry grass,
with a little sunlight and shadow to amuse you.

Go ahead! The walkway through the yard
was swept just yesterday. And to the west,
way back beyond the distant grove of maples,
way back right on the horizon, barely visible
in blue haze, is a hilltop of sorts
where your only neighbor, a Buddhist monk,
spends the whole day whittling sticks into tiny
rabbits. Who knows, maybe in a hundred years
you could journey there and introduce yourself.
But for now, no one even knows you're alive.

Well, it'll be getting dark soon,
and you'll have the entire night to yourself.
Of course, there's plenty of beer
in the refrigerator, and nachos with chili peppers.
The moon will be beautiful, as always,
coming up over the silhouette of the distant
trees, just before the immense appearance
of the stars. And, oh yes, I almost forgot,
there's pencils in the drawer and paper
if you care to write something, a poem or whatever.
And finally, when you're inside, keep the window
by the reading chair open. In fall,
you'll enjoy the tarnished air scented
with decaying leaves, and, in winter, that branch
there sways so gently, you'll want to cry.
In summer, try listening to the inaudible

tick of sunlight on the old wood
of the house, or the occasional late shower
in the afternoons. And, at night,
when it's windy, there's the weeds that bend
and rustle and do not whisper your name.

THE BULL GOD

The bull god moves from sunlight
Into shade, following the drool of his snout
To what he needs. Day after day the rhythm
Of his blood consumes him, his enormous
Body a gentle blue desire.

He stands for hours
In the August sun, flies weaving
A dark crown above his massive head
As he waits for the next flutter of delight
To stir the heavy neurons of his brain
And start again the oblivious lumbering
From pleasure to pleasure. The long
Slow nerve of his body touched
By the scent of bulrushes and black mud.

And rubbing against the half rotted
Post of a fence the coarse hide of his
Ponderous belly, he walks slowly away
Into the insect-singing heat, his great balls
Swaying behind him like heavy stones,
His ancient, swaggering cock as tense
With seed as a milkweed pod about to burst
With the next touch of the wind.

Farm Girls Unloading Tomatoes from a Pickup

I stop at the old farm before
going to work, looking for fresh tomatoes
to take for lunch and maybe
a bag of peaches. In white shirt and tie
(my jacket left in the car) I walk
to the wooden stalls, poking around
the bins of gracious fruit
and the crisp wet greens of rhubarb,
spinach and five or six varieties
of lettuce, loitering in the vegetable shade,
enjoying the flowery scent of melons
and red plums.

And through the back
entrance they arrive, lugging in
the bushels of new tomatoes, their tanned
arms straining with the bright weight.
Sixteen, maybe seventeen, hair loose and tangled
from labor, they move, bringing the grace
of flesh into the morning air. One
is blond, wearing a red sleeveless blouse
and cut-off jeans. Another, perhaps
the youngest, has on a green tee-shirt
with a large oval hole showing just under
her arm. Now the third one enters,
tall, dark-haired, strong. She swings her bushel
effortlessly up and lets the big tomatoes

tumble softly into the bin. I watch as she wipes
her forehead with her wrist, brushing back
her hair as she points and instructs
the others to unload—a line of dirt
marks her brow as she stands catching
her breath. Her white cotton blouse
is open a bit, tied in a loose knot
above her beltless cutoffs. And I notice,
as she turns, on her bare thigh, the wet
seeds and juice from a crushed tomato.

O Daughters of Gaea! Soiled Graces
of these fading Jersey farms! I love you
in this moment, the dirt on your hands,
the fertile grit and sweat on your necks—
something of old Hesiod remaining here
in these tailored suburbs this morning
as the cars flash by in the sunlight.
And though I know tonight I'd find you in make-up,
drinking a Coke in front of the Seven Eleven,
or smoking a cigarette in your boyfriend's
leering Firebird, for now I take you as vision
and pay for my bag of tomatoes, turning to look
once more as you walk back to the pickup;
knowing when I unwrap my sandwich at my desk,
under the sunless glare of fluorescent lights,
the first taste of this muscular red fruit
will enliven me again with this momentary
fragment of a myth.

THE LAST GOAT IN BERGEN COUNTY

O Master of humbleness!
Master of the ancient baaah!
Companion of Plato and Jesus,
Eater of boots and tin cans!
Is this how you end up,
On a little hilltop amid the noise
Of rush hour traffic, standing
Undignified, like a god in long
Underwear locked out of heaven?

Uncouth Old Testament
Prophet of barnyards and meadows,
Your dainty mouth and teeth
Tugging the short grass and nibbling
The fence posts. Can it be,
Right here amid the industrial parks
And corporate plazas of New Jersey,
Your frank manure still sweetens
The air, your hooves clattering
On these stones?

Each day, driving past,
I watch your stringy wisdom-beard
Blowing in the breeze of passing cars,
Wondering what you may be thinking,
Hobbling around, indifferent
To snow and rain and heat. Are you

Lonely up there? Do you dream
Of sunlight on the hills of Sicily
And the taste of olive leaves?
Or even those starched Dutch farms
That not long ago right here
Still heard in the humid mornings
The shiny clank of milk buckets?
Is that why
You stand so still?

Dream on, Old Knobby Knees,
Dream on. And in your goat thoughts
Recall those brighter days of Arcady
And those ancient nights of lust
And fluted music, when shepherds
Slept undaunted on the hills,
And the mad god Pan, ugly as sin,
Shook the endless woods with noisy dancing.

No Wife, No Kids, No Work

I wake alone
And throw my rested arms
Across the bed.
Not a sound in the house—
The floor is still asleep
Dreaming it is the ceiling.
Opening and closing
My eyes, I float for a long time,
Basking like a turtle
On the sea of late sunlight.
Later, wearing slippers
And a frayed blue robe,
I cook my breakfast.
In the sunlit, empty kitchen,
I feel like dancing
To the great silence. With a fork
In one hand and a cup
Of fragrant tea in the other,
Restored to a separate
Life, I stand at the stove
And watch as the eggs
Fry wildly in the noisy butter.

READING BASHO'S TRAVEL SKETCHES

Although it's summer I drink hot tea
To stay awake long enough to finish reading
Basho's travel sketches. Wherever
He goes, he is moved by his experience of things:
Visits to ruined temples, sleeping in barns,
Sharing a room innocently with two prostitutes;
Even his sadness at missing the full moon
At Kashima Shrine, or falling off his horse
Crossing Support-Yourself-On-A-Stick Pass.
How his warm eyes must have brightened finally
Under the brim of his worn out hat
As he beheld at last the wild cherry blossoms of Yoshino.

"Eternity," he always seemed to be saying, "is just
 Being somewhere with all of your heart."

Moose Love

Almost shyly the large male moves
slowly towards her,
his love
a patient bawling
of desire. He waits
with his big eyes open and calm,
days sometimes, for her
leisurely acquiescence
to his need.

He shakes from time to time
the two immense wings of his antlers,
rattling dry brush
and scraping the bark of trees;
a tense serenade, as she
walks on ahead,
her inviting rump flagrantly
casual of his arousal.

Only then, after such
meek pursuit and love-wandering,
finally, in the high weeds
of autumn, will she let him mount;
his great shaggy patience
brimming over into awkward passion,

as each long pulse of seed
fills her quietly
and she wears above her
the vast triumphal
wavering of his crown.

Nobody Knows the Answer to This Poem

Why is it sometimes just towards evening
when the sun is a sweet cool light over your house,
and maybe it's mid-spring and the trees
are that brief shade of green they only remain for a week;
that suddenly all of your doubts vanish for an instant,
and everything—your wife and children, the shoes
you are wearing, the garage full of junk, your hands—
seems blessed, though nothing in your life has changed
except there's this light you are part of,
this light making everything clear, so all you have suffered
and all you will suffer, even your mother's death
from cancer and your own death to come and the death
of all that you love seems perfect; and the light
shines right through your chest and into your heart
leaving only this happiness for a wound?

POETRY IS THE ART OF NOT SUCCEEDING

Poetry is the art of not succeeding;
the art of making a little ritual
out of your own bad luck, lighting a little fire
made of leaves, reciting a prayer
in the ordinary dark.

It's the art of those who didn't make it
after all; who were lucky enough to be
left behind, while the winners ran on ahead
to wherever it is winners
go running to.

O blessed rainy day, glorious
as a paper bag. The kingdom of poetry
is like this—quiet, anonymous,
a dab of sunlight on the back of your hand,
a view out the window just before dusk.

It's an art more shadow than statue,
and has something to do with your dreams
running out—a bare branch darkening
on a winter sky, the week-old snow
frozen into something hard.

It's an art as simple as drinking water
from a tin cup; of loving that moment
at the end of autumn, say, when the air
holds no more promises, and the days are short
and likely to be gray.

A bland light is best to see it in.
Middle age brings it to flower.
And there, just when you're feeling your weakest,
it floods you completely,
leaving you weeping as you drive your car.

Anima Mundi

And her knees
Have no forgiveness

Reclined in the vast leisure of the sun
Naked, she closes her powerful eyes
Remembering the men her legs have tasted.

Resting at last from desire
All afternoon she spends eternity asleep
With the uncreated—a blue wasp

Glittering on her luminous finger
Like a ring.

WEEDS

Horseweed, Quackgrass, Creeping Jenny . . .
Goosefoot, Beggar's Lice, Bachelor's Buttons . . .
These days it seems I have more interest
In the names of weeds than in the breasts
Of women. Their homely titles remind me
Of the early Ch'an Master Shui Liao
Whose name also means "a small dirty pool
Of rain water along the road."

Ribwort, Pigweed, Fleabane,
With my children trailing behind me, I wander
The yard and beyond, spending the afternoon
Searching out the names of these ragged
Little monks. By evening, I put down my pocket
Guide to weeds and wait on the porch
For darkness. Suddenly, a poem comes to me
Out of nowhere and I write it down on the front
Page of the book:
    In the poverty
    Of a single weed, the solitude
    Of a thousand mountains.

SONG OF THE TULIP TREE

I stand alone
in my great height.
I cherish nothing

more than my own roots.
The decay of the world
is my nourishment.

What happens below me
passes like the floss
from autumn milkweed;

And the stars
Are no more than the hum of gnats
tossing in the vault

of my summer shade.
Not death not grief
not the thunder of human history

sway the vast and wrinkled
stone of my trunk.
My joy is in the sun

and the rain and the passionate
art of the wind
stirring like a lover

the enormous green play
of my branches.
What dies beneath me

finds no pity,
but in time is taken up
and sent out briefly to dance:

a nameless leaf in the wide
blue music of the weather.
And you, far below,

with your small face
looking up, I have no need
for homage.

Your human heart
is no more to me than a sparrow's
egg blown from its nest.

But if sometimes
out of loneliness or a desperate
urge to praise

you would seek me out,
then press your faint hand
reverently against

the ancient hide of my bark.
In a hundred years
your touch will travel through

each ring of my immense
armored heart, to tell me
you were here.

RAINING WITH THE SUN OUT

For the past half hour it's been raining
With the sun out. From the front porch
I stand watching as the weather confuses
The woman walking her dog who can't adjust
To the starting and stopping of this funny
Gentle rain. And my neighbor's wife comes out
To dump her bag of garbage and rushes
Back in as the rain comes down harder. Even
The ball game across the street is confused,
The outfielders looking up, one with his hand
Out and hat off, trying to decide if it's
Raining or not. Only two teenage girls, hair
Dyed blonde and wearing tight faded jeans,
Don't seem to mind, talking to each other
Nonchalantly, their heavy make-up barely
Disguising their underdeveloped breasts, or
The self-conscious way they blow their cigarette
Smoke out in mid-sentence. Their gauzy blouses
Have soaked up enough rain and stick delicately
To their arms and shoulders. I watch as they walk
Past me without even a glance in my direction,
Leaving a faint pleasing scent of cigarette smoke
And perfume. And turning, convinced finally
That it is raining, I go back into the house
Remembering again how I've been hungering all day
For my wife's sweet cunt and haven't been able

To get near her, knowing, too, it'll be a while
Before I do, the way she's so intent on finishing
Her work, and the kids indoors because of the rain.
And back inside, I walk up behind her
As she bends to pick up something in the kitchen
And rub up against her generous, soft ass,
A hard-on forming quickly in the crotch
Of my jeans. But she chides me and tells me
To go away, which I do, knowing after fifteen years
When it will happen and when it won't. And
Tenderly nursing my lonely married desire,
I go quietly out into the yard and walk
Where the big red tomatoes ripen slowly in neat rows
In the garden, where it's still raining
With the sun out.

AN OLD MAN IN COLD WEATHER

It was only a bus
He missed

Standing there stuttering "I missed
My bus."

Holding a plastic bag
Full of clothes in his arms

You could tell
He was crying his terrified

Voice "my bus my bus"
Putting the bag down

Stunned
His white hair every which way

In the snow.

LEAVES LIKE OLD BOARDS

The leaves are gone like the boards of an old barn
finally fallen away. Looking through branches,
it's as if the earth has something final to say about leaves
and about barns and the owners of barns,
and the cows and horses who snuffled to their names once
tossing their sluggish heads in the cold.
And each year the leaves add their weight to the world,
making the earth heavier, and each year we walk
wading through tides of leaves, snuffling a few times
in the cold, watching as what's left of the sun
fills the branches of the voiceless afternoon.

The barn and the leaves are gone.
The horses and cows and the owners of the barn are nowhere
to be found. Out there, among the dismantled trees
and the few broken windows of the weather, the wind
is the only tenant. And we, in our turn, are the farmhand,
or the ghost of the farmhand, playing our part for the season,
reaping, in the solitudes of a faded household warmth,
these last emotions amidst the clatter of everything fallen,
the sun on the fence, and these scant leaves
that hang, apple-red, in the barnlight.

Reading James Wright's Last Book

I sit down alone under a tree in the backyard
And read the last poems of James Wright.
Afraid for the book to end, I stop a long time
Between each poem, and when I have finished
Two or three, I go back and read them again, aloud,
Letting the voice reveal whatever my eyes had missed
The first time—that harsh, compassionate voice,
Defeated beyond defeat, moving tenderly over
The broken landscapes of Italy and grim Ohio.
And what I feel is a public loss, part of nature;
Like the way we'll all feel when they tell us
The last Great Blue Whale has sounded for the last time
And the whole sea is empty that day . . .
"Good-bye to the living place," he says at the end
Of the poem on page 18, "and all I ask it to do
Is to stay alive." And there, on the clean white space,
An ant climbs up the edge of the book
And enters the page.

LATE NOVEMBER AFTERNOON, FALLING ASLEEP IN A CHAIR WITH A HANDFUL OF BASIL SEEDS IN MY SHIRT POCKET

All day leaf mulch
Stained the air like rotting apples.
Slouched in my reading chair
Near the window, still wearing my hat,
I fall asleep and breathe in slowly
The pungent, windy fragrance of basil seeds
I stripped from the dead stalks
In the garden.

And outside, a sturdy wind
Blows late sunlight across the twiggy fields—
Rusted stems of chicory
And wild parsnip, amber filaments
Of goldenrod and Queen Anne's lace,
Fragile pepper grass and spiny winter cress—
The dense complexity
Of summer reduced to a simplicity
Of brown weeds.

Now the short days please
The spirit with a generous solitude,
And everything is a plainness
That satisfies—textures of bark and rock,
The sluggish stream glinting in curves through the blanched

Meadow, the bramble's rough sheen
In the aging sun. And somewhere further back,
The swaying bull thistles empty their milky heads
Into the wind—a joy of unburdening
Like the luxury of speechlessness
And untroubled sleep.

In the shriveled garden,
One soft gray tomato hangs from its stalk
Like a soggy weight, and the long
Shadow of the house deepens over the yard.
In the remaining light, the ripe scent
Of basil fills my sleep, and the crows
Call down the coldness
From the hills.

THE CORNER

This is my spot—
This corner of the yard
Overgrown with weeds
Near the woodpile
And the compost heap.
All summer long
It molders with a lyric
Rot, moldy woodstink
I feel at home with;
Where the cowish slugs
Graze in the moist decay,
And shy colonies of woodlice
Sleep in eternal peace
Under the weathered logs.
—A joyful neglect
I make my small defense
Against the advanced
Barbarians of precision
And order . . .

   And here,
In the afternoon, resting
In an old lawn chair
After gardening,
I am lulled by the bleary
Disorienting sun,
The green bluebottle flies

Magnetized on and off the compost heap;
The sweet smell of summer
Sweat under the brim
Of my pulled down
baseball cap.

And sometimes,
Sitting into the evening,
I listen as the marsh
Begins its froggy music,
Threatening with its clicks
And drones, as a hundred
Million insects rage
With biological intensity,
The steady racket beckoning me,
Like the old gods,

Back through the swaying ten foot grasses,
Into the soft body of the marsh
To lose myself in the dark
Fur of night.

.   .   .

In winter, too, I sit here;
The chair frozen,
The fragile sunlight glimmering
Off the woodpile quiet under
Old snow. Sometimes,
Bringing out a cup of warm sake,
I watch the pungent steam
Rise into the clear air

And with the first slow sip
Give up all thought, surrendering myself
To the precise fragrance
Of the cold, the sun making paradise
Behind my closed eyes.
Or just as it begins
To snow, I watch as the flakes
Fall with a heavy, increasing
Silence, and throw back my head,
Feeling each tiny wetness
Like a blessing, a sort of
Snowy lovemaking, as they fall
On an open human face, getting caught
In my lashes and nose hairs—
Tiny benedictions we only receive
When we sit in the cold or heat
For its own sake, surrendered at last
To bug and weed and weather.
And when the snow has covered me,
I get up carefully, trying to keep
From losing the pure white coat,
As I walk slowly back to the house,
The children at the kitchen window
Laughing at my approach.

At the End of Day

When the sun
Deepens at the edge of the sky,
And evening
Takes down the houses . . .

When the world
Under so many shadows
Tips a little nearer to its vanishing;
And the car I drive,
Battered with ten years traveling,
Parked in the long light,
Sweetens inside
With tobacco and spilled beer . . .

I walk out, in a coat
Woven from the clear voice of my wife,
And standing, feel the pulse
Of my life shut down,
And lift a black flower, the shadow
Of a single tree, and hold it
Until everything
I have had to touch to stay alive
Takes its unfinished place.

My Dream of the Pure Land Paradise

When I'm finally reborn
Into that Western Paradise, I want to spend
My infinite kalpas hauling lotus blossoms
For the Buddha. And making my way
Across the radiant plains of Heaven,
Country-Buddha music playing on the radio,
I'll smoke a thousand cigarettes a day,
My elbow hanging out the window
Of the cab, trying to make the Pure Land
By sundown tomorrow, knowing always
The Master's Everlasting-Compassionate-
Pure-Shining-Unfathomable-Perfect
Smile awaits me there.

Every-Minute-Zen

Moment to moment our attention
should be at least the same as when
we approach an angry hornet
that's gotten into the house and we move
slowly towards it with a rolled up
magazine, hardly breathing, giving ourselves
just this one chance.

Last Poem

The lizard clamped to his rock
Who waits, patient with his life, and as green
And cool in the sun as a blowing leaf . . .

The ant, by itself, stumbling forward
Steady and direct and without belief
Over the crumbling sand . . .

And the sea turtle who sleeps
Afloat on the sea. You too. Your little feet
Always pushing against the endless . . .

Or the killifish in Africa, so tiny,
Swimming its lifetime in the rain-filled footprint
Of an elephant . . . You too.

And you crab, and you barnacle and slug;
Silverfish, caterpillar, snake . . . You too.
And the peaceful sponge

And the cranefly who dances
On air . . . You too.

Snail

The sea
that left you here
is gone.

Poking
only the air now
with your soft

minuscule feelers,
you have learned to survive
on the thinnest

of mists—
on a leaf glazed
with morning

or the moist
sea of evening air.
Thick-footed,

patient these
hundred million years
or so,

you still hold
your last watery breath
inside the deepest

spiral of your
ear-shaped shell,
sipping, one molecule

at a time
your microscopic drink
from the trough

of a clover leaf.
Yet with what gratefulness
you set out each dawn

past twig and pebble
headed for the great
wet rock in this meadow

or poised on a shining
grass blade
waiting and waiting

—yet never in a hurry—
for that sea
that abandoned you

to return. Ah
patient little brother,
at noon

when you sleep
in the last dampness left
under an old leaf

keeping your perishable
life safe
from that alien sun

is it the faint
echo of that vanished surf
your heartbeat follows?

ELEGY FOR WILLIAM LEBO

Skinny William Lebo,
My grade school friend.

I remember still how you hated
Being called Willy, and insisted,
Though it was useless,
That your name was Bill.

It's strange how I find myself
Thinking of you here
Some thirty years later
At this Christmas band recital,
Watching as my kids play in the school
Auditorium, filling the room
With their off-key,
Sour chromatics.

Skinny William Lebo,
Skinny and dark skinned,
With your glasses taped along one arm
And always sliding
Down your nose.
Skinny William Lebo. Your crew cut
In summer making your ears
Stick out even more.

But somehow we never
Laughed at you, even though your clothes
Were poor and you were always first
To be out playing dodge ball;
Or when you didn't do your homework
And Sister Alice, that tormentor
Of the souls of boys,
Ridiculed you till you burst
Into tears in front of us,
And you couldn't stand still,
Red-eyed, humiliated,
Martyred to that same ambiguous
Authority we all dreaded.

"And stop that silly dancing
When I speak to you."
But you couldn't, and she slapped
You again, your skinny body
Shaking, rocking from foot to foot,
Fragile in your awkward pants
And wrinkled shirt.

Skinny William Lebo.
All your troubles—homework lost
Or incomplete, tests flunked
Endlessly, broken glasses, plain
Dumbness. I can still see
Your oversized, illegible handwriting,
The paper half blank, worn and crumpled

Covered with tiny rolled crumbs
Of soap eraser.

But there was no bravado,
No heroics. It was desperation
Kept you going. You had no choice
But cling to what dignity you could,
Wrinkled clothes and all.
And that day you let fly
Your skinny rage, swinging wildly,
Hitting Sister with your hat,
You couldn't put up with it
Anymore, and she dragged you off
Weeping and yelling to the office.

Skinny William Lebo.
You were my friend a while,
Sometime between third and fifth grades
Before you disappeared
Sometime between sixth and seventh.
We thought it was all that trouble
And bad grades finally got you
Kicked out. But then,
Months later, there were rumors
About public school, and then
Something about illness.

All I remember is
It was summer when we'd heard you died;

Some spinal disease, some unknown
Ugly sickness. Even now
I don't know what it was. I remember
It was during baseball when someone said
"William Lebo's dead." But by then
You were already a ghost to us,
Gone from the daily life
Of school and play. I remember
Being too busy to feel very mournful
At the time. But now,
During this litany of sour notes
And squealing clarinets,
I feel that mournfulness. The big empty years
Your parents must have had
Full of grief, that we never even thought of,
But I think of now, as I listen
To this music, so broken and innocent,
A troubled, tender music like the suffering
Of childhood we barely dare
To remember anymore.

O skinny William Lebo,
Forgive us, if you can!
While you were dying that summer
We were sliding into third, or maybe
Racing bikes down Taggart Way,
Or walking home from fishing
Moody and grumbling over having to eat.
All that clear, young summer,

What was it like for you, by yourself,
Not even your old classmates knowing
The sour history of your life.
O skinny William Lebo. I'll always
Remember your sweet spirit and dignity
Against all odds, your desire
For true friendship, your sad
And gangly presence, and your painful
Dumbness that we all understood
And forgave you for. I hope
There is a heaven, at least for kids like you.
Some place safe from ugly death
And spinal diseases, and rancid nuns
Who never knew your beauty, William Lebo.

THE GOOD MORNING

For no reason
one morning you are
up early. The sun
is there and green leaves
sway together
at the open window.
From perfect sleep
your eyes open
without effort,
and rising, your whole
body, bones and muscles,
moves with the blood
through your heart.
You have never in your life
moved this way before,
It's as if suddenly
someone else is controlling
your hands and feet,
or it's your body
thinking for itself.
And light with hunger,
your body takes you
to the kitchen for breakfast.
And everything is alive
there as never before:
the two blue chairs

stand in their space
like giant birds,
and the table too
has become a tall mushroom
where the book you left
out last night face down
sleeps in its color
like a butterfly.
And then you do
what you have never
done before
and sit down on a giant
bird, leaning your
elbow on a mushroom,
turning the wings
of a red butterfly,
while the whole time
a white cup
filled with black coffee
stares up at you
like the curious eye
of a hen.

Sick Day, Home with the Flu

Leaning on my pillow, away from the office . . .
At last I understand that in the service of the state
It is only in sickness that a man has leisure.

Po Chu-i (772–846)

In no big hurry now
and feeling far from the world,
I fix a gentle lunch
of hot broth and tea,
sipping contentedly at the kitchen table.
Later, still weak and chilled
with fever, I sit outdoors
on the back porch in the clear autumn weather.
Wrapped in my long winter coat to keep
from chattering, and reading a few pages
of the Nirvana Sutra, I stop
from time to time to blow my nose
in a big red-flowered handkerchief.
But after a while I can't resist any longer—
Getting up, I walk out in the yard towards a patch
of dry grass the sun has kept warm
all morning, and stuffing my hands into my coat pockets,
I lie down right there, stretched out
like a bum on the hard ground.
And lying still, my big coat
keeping me warm, I close my eyes
and feel my feverish face glow in the noon warmth

like a disk of pure light—
drifting into a deep red sleep under falling leaves,
until I wake—my wife calling me
from the back door
to come inside.

After Working

I return home
Near morning. Exhausted,
I still carry in my hands the faint
Hum of the steering wheel.
My wife is asleep, one arm
Under the pillow. Already
Gray light is breaking into the room—
It kneels
To her sleeping hand.

Bitter with failure and fatigue,
I open myself
Now and let in
The breath of this woman,
Which has been filling the room
In my absence.
It enters my body to make me sleepy,
And I lumber into bed
Beside her not bothering
To take off my clothes.
Alone, my hand
Finds its way to her hair
As if it had been lost for a long time
And is come home at last.

As the room brightens,
The objects of our lives

Take shape.
I shift my weight in the bed,
look into her sleeping face.
A soft eye
Opens.

SATURDAY

The whole day my wife and I
Fight over everything that happens;
Our black words dart like bats
Through every room in the house,
By evening, the loneliness of it all
Comes over me like a drug. When I pick
My daughter up for a hug, she wraps me
Tight in her arms and doesn't
Let go for a long time.

ODE TO SATURDAY

O praise
This day named
Saturday! I wake
To sunlight the color
Of butter, a square of it
Across the sheets.
Under her flannel nightgown,
My wife's soft breast,
The nipple flesh
Visible as she sleeps.
All week it seems
I have been in a dream and now
Wake up to weather
And this private silence
That keeps me sane.
The energy of night
Has stiffened my cock,
Awakened its longing
To bury itself in that holy
Softness. But not yet,
Let her sleep. Instead,
Nuzzle close to that unarmored
Breast fragrant with milky
Flesh scent. Let sunlight
Close my eyes again.
Sleep. O praise
This day named Saturday.

ONLY HERE

I wake
Holding the blue piece
Of a dream. And lying still
On the cloudy pillow,
Before the day's first word
Spreads meaning out over the world,
I let the morning rain
Be all I am.

And in the slender
Stone-colored light, the ordinary
Promises of my life are made again,
Attaching themselves silkenly
Like rain to the window
Or my car glazed like a white rose
In the driveway.

And the dream
Now cold, blows away
Like history, my wife
Stirring beside me, the feathery touch
Of our first child turning
In her widening belly. Downstairs,
The kitchen waits. There is nothing
To decide. Everything asleep
Is about to awake, the day
Set like a mighty clock
In the silence.

Opening our eyes,
We lift the world; the universe
Tossed like rain from the tips
Of our lashes. Only here
Our ordinary eyes learn to find eternity—
There is nothing else. The luster
Is this plainness we walk in;
This poverty we rise to
At the end of dreaming—
The sacrament each day
Of our feet touching
The floor.

THE SALT OF GOD

Touch immense and unshakable.
Enormous, the smell of it piled in the sun like fish.
Mouths, olives and silk;
Trains colliding again and again into softness.
Even sleep has the odor of shoes;
Whispers thick as the breath of horses shudder like moths
    in the room.
Over and over with its tongue pressed to your eyelid
Fade, dissolve, taste into the knee
Of an endless and vanishing woman.

FOR MY MOTHER

This love is now complete.
This flesh returned to sky,
This bone to cloud.

After grief, the lungs are brighter;
A pair of wings for flying deeper.
In time all sorrows return to wind,
As glass to sand.

"What began will come to an end.
What is wonderful is not threatened."

Outside, on the bare winter field,
All morning the snow falls
Into the open arms of the weeds.

Deep Snow

Of the day
Only silence is left. Outside,
The snow sheds its feathery, dry leaves,
Climbing slowly down
Out of the dense night, building
A stillness

In white branches.
And we watch from windows now
The earth
We no longer own; our cars
Slipping away under
Such heavenly weight,

All day we trudged
And dug, our heavy shoes keeping us
To the shifting ground
As we puffed out each sharp breath
Against the cold,
Our muscles

Hard and spiritual
After the new work. Or holding
Shovels, we rested, dazed
And pillowed, our eyes
Weighted with too much light.
But tonight

We stand still,
Anxious and a little wild
Without the daily speed
Of forward. And knowing a bare need,
We watch (growing larger,
Childish before sleep)

The demon plow
Working the slow road
Into tomorrow; huge white piles
Like angels sleeping
On the world. How much of heaven
It takes to hold us
Earthbound, to our lives.

TRANCE

Early summer—
under the shadow of a single maple leaf
this little kingdom without hammers.

STAYING HOME FROM WORK AGAIN WITH A BAD BACK

O happiness of utter solitude!
O joyfulness of eating all alone!
The summer yard surrounds the house with its green love.
The peanut butter and jelly stand on the table like a great feast.
What more of gladness does a man need to know than to spend
    a day in his house by himself,
Listening through the open windows to the breezy swish
    of passing cars,
The tiny clangs of workmen building something far away,
The lazy muffled drone of a passing plane,
The long wave of maple leaves shimmering in the yard.
And I am happy, unquestioning, dazed somewhat like a boy
    with his hair still tousled from sleep.
And deep within there is a faint yet wonderful urge to weep,
    though I don't, but I know what I would be weeping for
    if I did.

After lunch, the kitchen is a kingdom of sunlight and silence . . .
The faded linoleum floor is like the face of an old friend . . .
And I feel as if I have almost disappeared, alone like an ant
    wandering far from its nest and carrying nothing.
And I am certain now this life is only a fleeting dream
    in the mind of a god we have all forgotten—
    the God of Happiness.

Epithalamion / Night Drive

All night
Speed and darkness through Pennsylvania,
The car taking us home
Lopsided, the back seat full of clothes.

Drowsy near Hazleton, we talk;
A diesel truck pulling close along side
Shaking our voices.
At the gas station, the damp air wakes us
With its wild smell.

Rain in the Alleghenies.
A moth flutters into the windshield.
Everything now is a beginning.
Leaning against the window you fall asleep
In the small glow of the dash board.

We move like a candle through the black hands
Of the mountains.

The Bombs of Spring

At the resumption of US underground testing.

Buildings in Nevada shake—
The bombs of spring blossom under the earth.
In the desert, prairie dogs look up but cannot see
The invisible hawk gliding overhead on the wind.
In New England, seconds later, a cloud of starlings
Scatters from a tree, circles and then returns.
In Greenland, near dusk, a herd of caribou looks up,
A wave of silence traveling along their shaggy antlers.
And farther away, in Istanbul, a lizard sways on a tree
And blinks its slow eyes once in the sun.
And in Africa, a spider monkey chatters excitedly,
Shaking the monkey next to him in the tree.
In Romania, just outside Bucharest, a farm cow moos
And gets up suddenly, scaring the chickens.
And farther away, in Mongolia, a pony led on foot
Pulls back for no reason, its eyes flaring.
And in Australia, a single crumb falls loose from a termite nest
And tumbles to the ground unnoticed.
And somewhere in South America, in the deep peat
Of the forest, an ant stumbles carrying a fragment of leaf.
And farther away, in the Sierra Nevada mountains of California,
A slumbering grizzly paws at his nose and thinks it's a mosquito.

And on the porch of a house in Minnesota, a fly flits
From arm rest to arm rest on the wicker furniture.
And farthest away, in the White House, a pencil rolls by itself
Off the sleeping President's desk, and his dog scratches at the door
   whining to be let out.

In the Silence After Fighting

I sit in the kitchen
Drinking coffee.
At the door
You stand with your coat on,
Cursing into your pocketbook
For the keys.

Angry with the need
To apologize,
I make a wisecrack
To defend myself.

Then, triumphant,
You have found the keys.
Beyond words now
You strike back
With unstable laughter
And slam the door.

I punch
The saltines off the table.

A Sip of Blue

I stare down at the blank page
before me on the desk. And choosing a single word,
I take a sip slowly . . . Blue.
It is like the taste of a hundred
blue mountains; blue as an angel, a leaf;
like the sweet blue taste of a woman's tongue
gliding along my teeth.

In that one sip I can even taste
The frail spiritual despair of the evening light.

And when I put down the pen, the page
still empty, I sink into myself like a boy
gazing out over the flashing
blue shield of a lake, the sunlit water
slapping against his wet shoes.

Essay on Hair

What was once your proudest possession is now withering. Every man has a secret love for his hair, feels it as part of his indispensable womanliness. In youth he combs it the way a woman puts on a new dress, or carefully makes a bed in the morning. Stroking his hair is like feeling his own sleek erection.

But when a man starts losing his hair, he feels his powers begin to waver. And the more he loses, the deeper he understands that time exists. Each day, his inner self cries out to be set free. Losing his hair, a man begins to get frightened, and the angrier he becomes at his own boyishness. The more he loses, the deeper he must go into his own inner woman to find strength, and the more attached he becomes to the soft fragrant flesh of his wife's breasts.

Slowly, with each combful of fallen hair, a growing desire possesses him to invent something, like a new mathematical formula, or a new household appliance. Suddenly he feels himself drawn to and fascinated by powerful animals, and dreams at night of the extinct woolly mammoth. And the more he loses, the more he begins remembering unimportant dates like the last time it rained or the day he bought his last new car.

It is mysterious, this falling out of the hair. The more it falls, the easier it is for a man to agree to go to war or die in an automobile accident. And the more it falls out, the more real his sexual fantasies become, and the more willing he becomes to ask his wife point blank for sex. And the more it falls out, the safer he feels doing something dishonest like taking a bribe or cheating on his wife. And each day the thought "waste no more time" repeats itself over and over, and he is reminded of the fact that it's now twenty or thirty years since he promised himself he would give up masturbation.

But worst of all, the more hair a man loses, the more serious he becomes about his life, and he begins wondering what people are thinking of him, especially receptionists and stewardesses. And the more hair he loses, the more solemnly he goes about buying things like a new pair of shoes or a new snow shovel. And death seems more real to him now. Death that comes as a smiling bald man who scatters loose hair from a pouch like a grim Johnny Appleseed: black hair, blond hair, brown hair, red hair. Tossing up into the wind strands of all the lost hair of all the bald men who have ever lived: long Neanderthal hair and Cro-Magnon hair; long smooth Indian hair and curly African hair. Hair of chiefs and hair of slaves. Ringlets of Romans and Greeks, and the locks of 18th Century British scholars. And he shakes with terror as the bald reaper grins his bald smile and he recognizes strands of his own hair flying up out of Death's hand and a loud peal of bald laughter echoes through the night . . . . But worst of all, the more a man loses, the more he recognizes the need for pure solitude, but instead ends up watching a lot of television, and running his fingers again and again though his imaginary hair.

THE MAN WHO WAS AFRAID OF HAPPINESS

Once I was afraid of happiness.
I slept in a bed of ashes
to keep it away. In the morning,
I pulled down all the shades
and drank a glass of bitter tea.
Sometimes I set the radio
to pure static and hummed along.
When I felt lonely, I took out
my heart and scalded it with cold
water until it was numb.
At night, as penance before bed,
I stood for an hour on one foot
staring at my face in the bathroom mirror.
I was desperate to stay unhappy.
I had a portrait of Job in my living room.
I made a pact with the devil,
selling my soul for a lifetime
of unhappiness. At the first sign
of joy, I'd rehearse my elaborate
suicide plan: filling my mouth
with ice cubes, I'd sit by the phonograph
turning up the volume to Tom Jones's
"Delila" while I clicked an empty
revolver at my head.
To this day I don't know what drove me.

I was obsessed with being unhappy.
I paid others to help me do research,
and learned what I could from the Great Masters.
I studied all the techniques handed down
through the ages. I even paid money
for an unhappiness seminar.
But it was no use. In time my idealism
crumbled, and I became wonderfully depressed.
I remember the day it all ended.
It was autumn. I went outside in the yard
and stood under the falling leaves
holding an umbrella. I didn't
say a word. I knew it was over.
With the leaves falling around me,
I knelt and wept bitterly,
pleading for forgiveness.
Then I grew strangely calm.
I closed the umbrella and lifted my face
into the falling leaves and promised myself
I'd always be happy no matter what.
Absolutely nothing would stop me.
I went in the house and threw my life-size
statue of Buddha into the garbage.
Then I burned all my poetry.

I cleaned up the house and washed
all the dishes piled up in the sink
after so many years of unhappiness.
When I finished, every room was spotless.

Now each day I enjoy going to work,
coming home, watching television.
I'm amazed at how easy it is to be happy.
It's so simple it's almost impossible
to resist. Everywhere you look,
happiness! happiness! happiness!
And I never knew wearing a tie could be
so much fun. And how good microwave
dinners really taste. And I tell you,
now in the morning, I wake up ready
to face the day with a smile.
I've completely forgotten my old life.
And everyone is so happy for me.
I wish somehow I could convince you.

THE INVENTION OF IMMORTALITY

I had just turned
To go, when you called me
Back into your room
The lamp a velvety glow
Beside the bed.
"I love you" you said
To me, the words
Strangely stark and serious
In their familiar
Setting. And leaning
Over you, your small face
At four and a half
Just blossoming into boyishness,
You reached up and
Drew me down with such a
Frightening hug
Into your pillow, whispering,
"Even when I'm dead
I'll love you."

STILL LIFE

Warm Christmas afternoon.
After the gifts have been opened,
Dinner eaten . . .

Under an Easter blue sky with clouds,
Untouched for three years my mother's clothespin bag,
Weather eaten and beginning to crumble,
Still hangs on the line.

Near Midnight

I let go slowly the weight
Of another day. Leaving my scattered desk,
I open the window for a little air—

A new rain quiets the streets.
There is only the soft, splashing sound
Of a few cars driving past

On the avenue. And below me, suddenly,
A man's voice, so vivid
As I listen to him talking, saying good-bye

In the rainy night, until a car door
Slams shut and I'm alone again.
And I keep on listening, feeling the day

Running out, near midnight,
And the noises from outside coming in—
The whole, restful city

Like a woman's delicate hands
Over my ears; until even a siren, far off,
Thins out into a thread of spiritual

Music. And something is gone from inside me;
A ghost, or the days I have lived out
The wrong way. Something finally lifted.

And I feel weak, dreamy, like a small
Boy who has finished crying. And everything—
The cars, the rainy night, the man's voice

That still seems to be talking, still held
In the fine bones of my ears—tells me.
"Whatever it is you want, you will never have.

Don't be afraid. Give up. Give up."

Remembering Joe Salerno

It was a lively time for poetry at the University of Michigan in the early seventies. My friend Bert Hornback set up regular Tuesday afternoon readings, which were well-attended—a hundred at the worst, four hundred on good days. Robert Bly and Galway Kinnell came every year; Wendell Berry, John Logan, Denise Levertov, Adrienne Rich. Joe was always there—with David Tucker and other Ann Arbor poets. There were readings at coffee houses, bookstores, and bars. Poetry was both lively and ordinary.

Joe loved the "ordinary"—a favorite word in his poems—but he was not ordinary. He was outstanding in his talent and in his passionate love for the art of poetry. There were two ways to watch a poetry reading: one was to watch the reader; the other was to watch Joe's countenance, where the poems played themselves out. After the readings, Ann Arbor poets gathered to talk with the visitor. I remember Joe—intense and serious and tender—talking with John Logan. I remember Joe with James Wright.

Joe Salerno's devotion to poetry—to the art, not to himself as a practitioner—set a standard for everybody. When he and I saw each other, I felt renewed by Joe. If any cynicism or professionalism had stuck to me, Joe rubbed it away by his clear and radiant passion for the art itself. It is wretched that he died young, like his friend my late wife, Jane Kenyon.

The greatest characteristic of Joe Salerno's own poetry is love for the world of things, of flesh, and of language. His sensibility is amative and erotic. He wrote with the appetite of the body, expressed by the poet's joy in diction and cadence. Joe's poems collected here are better than the poems I saw in 1974, but he was already good then—and he was already reticent, shy about putting his own work forward. I wish he had been bolder. Remembering young Joe from twenty-five years ago, reading the mature work after his death, I need to list my favorite poems. If readers want to check Joe Salerno out, they must not miss "In the Heaven of Obscurity"—

> In summer, try listening to the inaudible
> tick of sunlight on the old wood
> of the house, or the occasional late shower
> in the afternoons. And, at night,
> when it's windy, there's the weeds that bend
> and rustle and do not whisper your name.

—or "The Bull God," "Moose Love," "Anima Mundi," and "Reading Basho's Travel Sketches"—where the final lines make me think of Joe himself:

> "Eternity," he always seemed to be saying, "is just
> Being somewhere with all of your heart."

Read "The Bombs of Spring," "At the End of Day," and "Only Here." Read Salerno *passim,* but be sure you *don't* miss "Raining with the Sun Out," "An Old Man in Cold Weather," "Poetry Is the Art of Not Succeeding," "The Good Morning," "Nobody Knows the Answer to This Poem," or the last poem here that ends:

> "Whatever it is you want, you will never have.
> Don't be afraid. Give up. Give up."

By giving up, by his art of "not succeeding," Joe has left behind a triumphant, sweet, and astounding book. Reading his poems we will continue remembering Joe Salerno.

—Donald Hall